# BLUE

*Love Letters to Fatima*

NORIAN LOVE

This is a work of fiction. Names, characters, businesses, organizations, places, events, and incidents either are the product of the author's imagination or used factiously. Any resemblance to actual persons, living or dead, events or locales is entirely coincidental.

© 2021 by Norian Love

© 2021 Project 7even Publishing

ISBN-13: 978-1-7366707-2-9

ISBN-10: 1-7366707-2-7

All rights reserved.

www.norianlove.com

# INTRODUCTION

Before we begin I want to let you know the reason I wrote this... journal.

Blue, isn't like any other book you've probably read. It's a collection of thoughts and feelings Tatum expressed to Autumn in the best way he knew how. An intimate glimpse into the mind of a man's heart while it was breaking. Some thoughts were complete, some were just passing thoughts but hopefully you will be able to see, ultimately it was his way of saying I love you, equal in expression to Autumn's self-portrait, Fatima. Having said that, enjoy it through the view of a person who stumbled upon the journal and the secrets of the heart it contains.

Norian

## I

## IT COULD ALL BE SO SIMPLE

Hey Fatima,
    I wasn't sure if you'd come to my graduation. I thought about mailing this to you but somehow, I knew this would be a day you wouldn't let slip away. I miss you daily, terribly, and I don't know how to stop thinking about you. I spend mornings remembering your touch and nights forgetting your kiss. It hurts because slowly you are becoming the most unfortunate thing a lover could ever have. A fond memory of what was. And that shit kinda haunts me. Just knowing what life has to offer but being... well deciding to do something else. This probably isn't the place for this question but I wonder, which one is love? Following your duty or following your heart? I wonder why, for me at least, they come in direct conflict with one another. So, this is my line in the sand. This is me not trying to justify what I've done, but for you to know how much you mean to me, despite everything that's happened. If you ever read these words, it's my hope that you have enough love in your heart to close your eyes and remember what it was like the last time or any time I looked into them and as we kissed, our souls danced and our bodies were joined as one. You'll know in this moment that I'm here with you, looking into your eyes with the promise of tomorrow, the hope of the future sealed with each thrust

into one another. I want you to remember that you are looking into my naked soul and when you open your eyes know I'm still in that very spot, madly in love with you because *this* was real and I don't think I'll ever be able to say that again in this life. My heart is in these pages for you to read until the end of our days.

I don't know if you'll ever read this, but it's only fair, I give this to you. These are the feelings in my heart. This is everything I've ever felt that matters.

If I could change things I would love you forever, and I think you know that. I don't want to get too wrapped up in emotion. I just wanted to thank you for the moments in my life, every pleasant day, every beautiful feeling, you made it all worth having...

I'll love you until the end of my days.


Forever,
   Blue.

## 2
## 8o8'S & HEARTBREAK

S~~o I'm not gonna do a whole bunch of monologuing.~~ You're in my heart so I'm gonna talk to you the way I talk to you. This right here was something I've thought about doing but I wasn't sure if it made sense. I want it to be a song. Oh I met a singer too. No, not Preston Cole though. There's so much we have to catch up on. Things are crazy, but where was I? I think I'm going to make this a song.

※

WHEN WE FELL IN LOVE, I GAVE YOU MY HEART.
    Girl, there is nothing I won't do for you.
    You're deep in my soul, I wanted you here... always.
    Then we fell apart, the road became dark,
    And even still then I wanted to be with you.
    I tried to move on, but then I realized,
    I never had a love like this.
    Girl, I was feeling broken.
    Just sitting at home hoping.
    That somehow you'd be open.
    To work it out or talk sometime.

NORIAN LOVE

>	I didn't want to be here,
>	Just fighting back all these tears.
>	Why did you have to leave me here?
>	Alone with all the fragments of my heart

Or something like that. I don't know...

## 3

# EVERYTHANG

I wanna know if she loves me for me.
    I wanna know is this all that we'll ever be.
I wonder if she knows,
I miss her and it shows.
I wonder if she cares,
I wish I was still there.
I wonder If she sees,
She brings the best out of me.
I hoping that she knows,
I'll never let her go.
My heart beats
Drums to the thought of her in my mind.
It just beats and it beats when I'm thinking about her,
She don't know that I'm nothing without her.
She's everythang.
Everythang, everythang, everythang.
My baby is everythang, everythang, everythang, everythang.
My woman is everythang, everythang, everythang.
My darling is everythang, everythang, everythang.
And I put that on everythang.

ǳ 4 ǳ

## THE FALL (AUTUMN LEAVES)

Thought what we had was love,
    Thought what we had was real.
Thought we could face anything life threw our way,
That's how you made me feel.
Thought everything was fine,
Thought maybe we had time.
But time doesn't wait on anyone,
And that is where we came undone.
I wish that I could tell you,
I never wanted anyone but you.
I always tried to show you,
Despite all of the things I put you through.
You were always on my mind,
Every morning every night,
And I'm just standing here
Fighting when I've been all out of fight.

## 5

# END OF SUMMER

I wanted to call this song Heaven or End of Summer but I wasn't sure what it would be called. I think you'd like the name End of Summer because it's a play on your name. Fuck all that, I think I'm gonna call it Heaven because if we had to play Connect Four over this name change, you'd lose. Seriously, why are you so bad at this game? Did you not learn it's just one more than tic-tac-toe? I mean, you're really horrible, Fatima. At any rate, here's the song.

**END OF SUMMER (OR "HEAVEN" - I DON'T KNOW YET)**

I LOVED AN ANGEL ONCE, SHE LOVED ME BACK. I DON'T KNOW WHY.
   And when she helped me off the ground, she taught me how to fly.
   The sky was blue and beautiful, the wind beneath my wings.
   I wasn't in my cage no more; she taught me how to sing.
   I saw the beauty of the world, the meaning of this life.
   She helped me see beyond the pain, she helped me ease my strife.
   I flew and grew and knew that mortals never get to fly.

I cherished every moment cause I'd never been so high.

Heaven must have sent you from the stars up above, a love that never felt so true.

I wanna tell you how I feel about your love, night and day I dream of you.

## 6

## SOLDIER OF LOVE

All is fair in love and war, love is a battlefield.
Those scrapes and bruises probably hurt. How does this battle feel?
Your heart is land-mined to protect, your heart's a battlefield.
To make it mine, I'm prepared to die. Love is a battle, feel?

## 7

## 1000 CLOCKS

When your moment in time turned away from you
And you had nowhere else to go,
You came to me.
Every day I woke up and did my best
And slowly put you back together from the harshness of living.
Carefully, I told you the most intimate tales,
I fed you strength, covered you with comfort,
And showered you with love.
And the moment you were strong enough, you were gone
Without a goodbye.
Now that your moment has come again,
And the world is yours
The one thing you don't seem to have
For me,
Is time...
Time for me to be what I loved being
To you.
Still,
Know that when the hour turns away from you again,
And the moment is no longer yours,

BLUE

I will be here.
Tools in hand to put you back together piece by piece
And restore you
And while I won't hear from you until that day,
I know that day will come.
Because even a broken clock is right twice,
And for you,
I will be one thousand clocks.

## 8
# ARMOR

I think I gave you something like this at the Paint & Sip but I can't remember. Anyway this one just got me to thinking about how durable we were... together. I was there to protect you and I liked it. A~~t any rate, gonna quit talking right now.~~

Armor doesn't break,
    Armor doesn't fold,
    Armor is something
    That's forged from the soul.
    Armor does not crack,
    Armor endures,
    Armor is certain,
    Cause armor is sure.
    What it guards is important
    What it guards is life.
    What it guards... it loves,
    So any test is alright.
    Armor does not break,

Armor remains true,
Armor protects love,
Because armor loves you.

## ❧ 9 ❦
# AUTUMN LEAVES II

I fell in love at the end of November.
    I knew that nothing else compared to you.
The way I felt, thought I'd feel that forever,
I'm saying this to memories of you.
Wish I could've been better for you when you needed.
I'm sorry that I let you down.
Didn't take what we had for granted,
Just always thought I'd be around.
I didn't mean to make you cry,
I didn't want you to say goodbye.
I didn't want to hurt you or desert you,
Gone in the blink of an eye.
I didn't want you to get strong.
So sorry you had to move on,
Because in reality, baby, we both know,
We were right where we belonged.

## 10

## BLUE BIRD, DEFERRED

I've held on to dreams for far too long,
    Should've let them be a while ago.
My heart wasn't listening,
When my realities told me so.
"No time, no place for dreaming, all this work to be done."
"You're a father, a brother, a fighter, a lover, an employee, a son."
So, I have a different relationship with the word we call, "blue."
Why Maya's caged bird had to sing, what Langston clearly knew.
Still, when stillness comes my way, every now and then I dream...
Imagine how that blue would look if I could only use my wings.

## ❦ II ❦

# THOUGHTS AT HERMANN PARK

I ~~don't want you to think this is going to be me just telling you all the fucked-up-ness of the last few months. I'm sorry about these scratch throughs too~~. I want it to be clean but sometimes my thoughts aren't , you feel me? I just... this place, the words you're reading, it's how I *feel*. I don't get to express that in the world. Not the way I can *here*. I don't know if that makes sense or not but that's just the way it is...

Do you remember the first date? If I can capture one day and have you paint it, that would have to be it. Going to the museum. Looking back on it, I'm pretty sure that was the moment I knew I was in love. Watching the leaves fall in Hermann Park while you laid in my lap on the bench and laughed about nothing in particular. It was... peace. Your beautiful curly hair nestled against my shoulder and I could smell the lavender of your shampoo like I'm holding it in my hand as you read this. I didn't know it yet, but it was the start of one of the most beautiful relationships I'd have the pleasure of being a part of. I remember the softness in your eyes. You were nurture. The way I watched as you smiled and the coolness in the air made your bottom lip quiver. Come to think about it, there is just so much detail in the way we fell in love. I remember it all. There are days where it's the only way I remember you. That smile and the cackle in your laugh. And our authenticity. Slowly walking nowhere, having a lifetime to get there, and the weather being cool enough to be close to one another. And when the days get lonely, and the nights get dark. I relive this day. It was one of the best days of my life. And I thank you for it.

BLUE.

## EVERYTHANG (PT II)

Wonder if she knows I love her more every day.
That she's always on my mind, and I'm here to stay.
I need to know, if in any way she feels the same.
If she don't feel the way that I feel, I can't handle the pain.
My heart beats, she keeps me up late at night.
When I wake up just know that I'm thinking about her,
When I sleep then I'm dreaming about her.
She's everythang.

## 13

# GENESIS

I was alone when I saw you, my future queen.
    The most beautiful thing I'd ever seen- On this star filled eve.
Didn't know what to call you,
Didn't know what to say,
The only thing I knew that I could do,
Was pray that you would stay.
Running around paradise chasing you- I did whatever it takes.
You were uncontrollable back then, made a couple mistakes.
So I made them with you - what else could I do?
Please understand all I was ever trying to do was protect you.
So we had to leave ecstasy, but that was ok.
Cause you were there right by my side, so we were on our way.
We were out in the wilderness, working hard all the time.
No matter what we had to do for food and shelter, you didn't seem to mind.
Me and you against the whole damn world, just a man and wife,
And on a night like the one where I met you- we created life.
We made a beautiful family; it brought its pleasure and pain,
But we endured it together no matter what and that's so hard to attain.

And I watched the wrinkles come over you as the time marched on,
    Holding hands until our golden years come and we both pass on.
    But before our next lifetime, there's something you should know.
    I didn't regret anything along the way cause I love you so.
    If somehow I could go back- do it all over again,
    You and me in front of the fig tree, in the Garden of Eden.
    I would gladly pick the fig... and these words are true,
    Because the thing that is so misunderstood is...
    My paradise is you.

## 14

## LONE

We should be together,
      Yet sadly we're apart.
But we are still together,
Because you have my heart.
Is it beating? Is it bleeding?
Am I breathing? Are you sure?
Is it working? Are you certain?
How much more must I endure?
How much malice must I manage?
While you have your way with me?
...I'll keep feeling all you're dealing,
Till you bring it back to me.

## AUTUMN LEAVES III

Forty-three hours since I've seen you last.
    Feel the pain looking through the rain-stained glass.
Just another sad clown sitting in a small car,
Looking at her picture, too proud to tell her I miss her.
But even with these covers, an empty bed feels cold.
Echoes of your laugh scrape against my soul...
No one ever tells you until you gain experience,
What leaves with a woman is the warmth of a home.
So now I'm alone...
Sharing all these thoughts with a glass of Patrón,
Trying to be resilient but I gave all my strength to my heart,
'Fore it left so my strength's now gone.
All I want to do now is rest my head
In the sheets and the covers of this ice-cold bed....

## 16

## PICK UP THE PIECES

Of the heart that you have broken.
      Took the love we had for granted,
Took me being here for token.
Keeping my head above the water,
And I can't say this any franker.
Right now I feel just like I'm drowning,
And I feel like you're the anchor.
I use to look at you with love,
See hopes and dreams of a tomorrow.
Now I look at you with hurt,
All I see is pain and sorrow.
Truth be told I thought we'd be together forever,
But now I'm blocking your number like we don't know each other.
Like I never kissed your lips or we didn't go together,
How'd you turn " a couple forevers" into an "eh... whatever"?
All this anger has me putting up my walls again,
Build them stronger so I can make sure they don't fall again.
You called 12 times to apologize. I blocked them all again.
Still... I'm looking at my phone, hoping you call....again.

## 17

# THE BALLAD OF J.C. MONEY

I'm standing at this funeral,
    Don't know what it'll do to me.
Over fifty years being captured inside of a eulogy.
Over thirty years he spent trying to get through to me.
And now ironically the pain of his death is killing me.
But still I'm at his funeral,
Can't get my words together.
A part of me knows a part of me has changed forever.
Another part of me is fighting this altogether.
Denying all of my senses, my daddy is gone forever.
But I'm standing at his funeral,
Explaining this to my son,
"He came to do God's work and God's work is finally done."
My mother rolling her eyes like what have you become?
Fighting the urge to jump in and say, "What has he ever done?"
That half of me keeps calling the other half of me a bastard.
Disregarding the fact that half of me is in a casket.
This kind of stress just makes me want to resort to drinking.
My demons in a bottle, and all that I keep thinking, is
I'm not at this fucking funeral.

Some of you are blessed to never know what I'm saying.
'Spirits' calling me while I'm praying,
But no amount of praying can take away the pain that I'm feeling.
Don't know if I want a drink to fight or embrace my demons,
Cause I'm standing at this funeral.
Pops, I hope that you understand .
That I'm fighting tears inside.
Would you judge me as a man?
Can't even ask him that question,
Is this part of the Lord's plan?
I don't know how to feel,
My emotions are lost and damned.
Cause I'm standing at this funeral...
These family beans I'll spill.
My aunt and uncle asking questions bout his will.
I can't even get a moment of silence, y'all need to chill.
I don't know if naturally he died or if they tried to have him killed.
I just know your last days shouldn't be this way,
And if it is, then I'd worry too.
Tell me what's a man to do?
None of it's understandable.
The man I'd ask bout these tasks, he just passed.
So no answers to none of the questions I just asked
Cause I'm standing at his funeral.

## 18

## THE MIDDLE OF THE FALL

You were just a girl I met,
    In the middle of the fall,
And now I can't forget you,
I can't concentrate at all...
Accidentally bumped into you,
Wasn't even going to speak,
But your smile felt so familiar,
Like it was custom made for me.
Like I've known you several lifetimes,
Maybe we even had a child.
And we were married on a Thursday,
It was all there in your smile.
I said excuse me, miss, I'm sorry.
You said no worries at all,
You were right cause I was with you,
In the middle of the fall.
I want to tell you that I love you,
You're the air that helps me breathe.
And I know that I just met you,
But I don't want you to leave.

Where you walk to I will follow,
And when you need me to, I'll lead.
I just want to be by your side,
Cause that's where I'm meant to be.
If you love me will you say it?
Will you kiss me? Will you call?
Do you feel the way that I do?
Will you remember me at all?
...Or are you just a girl I met
In the middle of the fall?

## 19

## THE END OF A SEASON

Autumn,

LET ME SAY THANK YOU. I WOULDN'T BE HERE IF IT WASN'T FOR you giving up a piece of your heart. I can and will repay the money but I know I cannot repay what you gave up in Fatima. This is the hardest letter I've probably ever had to write. You're by far the best person I've ever met which is saying a lot considering how much I couldn't stand you when we first ran into each other. I thought to myself, there was no way I could ever like this woman and love wasn't even in the sphere of reality. But, here I stand a man hopelessly in love with a woman I can't have. Thank you for the wonderful times we've had together. I didn't know how to smile before you walked into my life. Now it feels as if I may never smile again. You've left something special with me, the appreciation of beauty, the validation through humor, and a fine admiration of art.

Your artwork is some of the most breathtaking masterpieces I've ever seen. I don't know much about art, but I know beauty, and you are an amazing artist. Autumn, each stroke of the pen is like the flair that is between your eyes, the spark in between your lips, and the heat in between your thighs. Apart from Solomon and yourself, I've never seen anything more majestic. It makes sense really because you are a living breathing work of art. It all starts with your smile. How it forces your cheeks to the corners of your face and pushes your eyes to widen melts me every time. I wasn't alive before you met me. But the way you forced your way into my world and the way you dance through life inspires everyone around you to realize life is truly worth living.

You're air on a cold winter day, filling me with life and shock all at once. Every moment, every kiss, every late night is something that is etched in my soul and something I know will forever be with you as well, because no matter where my body is, you have my heart. And what is a life without a heartbeat? What is life without love? Anyway, before this gets too emotional, please keep painting because I can't wait to see your works in the Houston Museum of Fine Arts where I know they all will hang one day.

I LOVE YOU.
Always,
Tatum

## 20

## UNTIL (FOCUS)

Till late nights turn into daylight,
　　Till daylight turns to play fights.
Till play fights turn into next nights,
Till next nights turn into weeknights.
Till weeknights turn into our life,
Till just a date turns to save the date.
Till save the date turns to wedding cake,
Till wedding cakes turn to, "Baby, I'm late."
Till, "Baby, I'm late," turns into baby weight.
Till baby weight turns to a kid that is eight,
Till that kid that is eight suddenly graduates,
And he or she moves out leaving our house,
And comes home one day with his or her spouse.
Perpetuating the cycle of what love is about,
I will focus on you.

## 21

# SONG OF SOLOMON

It's like round the start of February and I'm in love with you,
    And I'm recollecting about everything that life's put me through.
    And slowly you're emerging and I understand.
    It was always about being a father and a better man.
    So you come out...you're not breathing,
    But I'm right there believing
    That everything's gonna be ok.
    And right then, you start screaming,
    Now you're scared out of your mind
    I take your hand say, "Everything's fine,"
    And you calm down so instantly... it's the voice you've heard all the time.
    We make eye contact and you hold on,
    And don't let go and you're so strong,
    And I can't believe that you're mine, so
    I start crying and this just goes on.
    Now, there's a thousand people around but
    Truthfully I don't hear a sound,
    Because my prince is here, my legacy, the one I'm giving my crown.

I hand you over to your mom, she's exhausted... slightly scared,
But she loves you and I do too and we're both getting prepared.
I swore I'd live for you, or die for you, and dedicated my life to you,
But God told me that all he really wants me to do was *try* for you.
Cause He'd handle the rest,
And right then I knew you were blessed.
So I told you I loved you and held you close to my chest,
I gave my all every day, I hope one day you'll understand.
That my joy is being your father watching you grow into a man,
Cause I love you.

## 22

## WINTER IS HERE

Our season is over, I wish this wasn't true.
      Cause all I wanted in my life was to spend the fall with you.
We had so many great times, each and everyone was new,
And even all the bad that came, was better cause of you.
Girl, you have my heart, please take it all with you.
Cause I won't love no one else, the way that l love you.
I tried to keep you from the storms, did all that I could do,
And every misstep that I took, was just to walk to you.
I tried to keep you from the storms, did all that I could do,
And every misstep that I took, was just to walk to you.

## 23

# MONIQUE'S BALLAD

You told me you loved me but that was just a lie,
And I fell for your deception looking in your pretty eyes.
I thought what we had was special and that you're one of a kind.
I was infatuated with you; you were playing with my mind,
I don't want to recollect this, but I guess it's finally time.
Drinking, listening to Sade asking me, "Is it a crime?"
Cause I know that you're a nickel, yet I treat you like a dime,
And that has nothing to do with your breasts or your...
It's no question that you're attractive- let's just say that from the start,
But then factor in the "1" that is the malice in your heart,
And if you add the two together, after that, then you divide.
Then the woman who's a "10" suddenly becomes a "5,"
And I was happy with that number cause my heart was damaged too.
It was different, but I convinced myself it complimented you,
Till I saw all of the drama and the hell you'd take me through.
You can't even be upset that I want no parts of you.
True I should have seen this coming, Kenley said you was a hoe,

But that was back when we were younger, I assumed that you would grow.

Introduced you to my son cause I thought you were the one,

Plus you told me that you loved me- girl, you told me that you loved me.

Seemed to only say those words when you wanted something from me,

Wasn't long after you'd say them that you'd then manage to hurt me.

Caught up in a vicious cycle, we'd always seem to recycle,

I'd keep giving you my heart... then you'd break it on arrival,

But this time it's best I leave cause now I'm fighting for survival.

My sanity's on the ledge, I'm really close to the edge.

I'm finally out your snare and I honestly don't care.

What you're doing with your life, guess you took this as a dare,

Cause you call me sometime later, cause you, "- need to clear the air."

And I foolishly listen because I think I want to hear,

And in a flash you undid everything I did to prepare.

Cause you told me that you loved me,

Girl, you told me that you loved me...

## 24

## JUMPING FOR JOY

One starlit night on a trampoline,
 We were in the air without a care in the world.
The joy on your face, infectious in nature, tagged me,
And as I jumped, my worries melted and then something happened,
Maybe not at first, maybe not altogether,
But slowly, like anything worth truly having,
I swear it happened.
It didn't feel like jumping anymore,
It felt like falling,
And with each leap it felt
As if I was falling more rapidly
Towards a destination I hadn't been before
And the beautiful part about it was you were falling with me,
One starlight night on a trampoline.
We fell in love.

## 25

# NOTHING LEFT TO SAY

Relationship's end. I've had to accept that. People move on. And while moving on makes me wonder how life looks without you, I get sad because I don't know if time is going to heal this one.

One thing I think we both know is no one will ever love you the way I do. No one knows how to. I've invested my heart into us and it's terrible because I know you did the same. "I'm sorry" doesn't begin to cover the damage I know I'm causing. I just don't see any way that makes sense.

You know what I'm going to say here. I don't think I have the heart to write it again. It hurts too much to know that I'm speaking to you. Maybe you'll never read this book. I don't even wanna be doing this shit, man... I don't want a life without us. I'm so torn and I end up in a place that doesn't do anything but go through a range of wishing I had never met you, to being thankful for every moment. But when I think about it long enough, I come to one valid conclusion. It was always, truly always, my hope to be lying next to you looking in your big beautiful brown eyes as you read the words of our history and know without question you have my heart. It's right here in this journal. And you can keep it, Fatima, I'm done with love. There's no one else I'd rather give my heart to than you.

NORIAN LOVE

Forever yours.
Blue.

## 26

# JOURNEY TO THE PYRAMIDS.

Remember the night I gave you the purple rose?
    I miss the well where we would sit and I could inhale you in indiscriminate ways.
  I know the temperature of your inner right thigh
and how much your left thigh shakes before your
Release.
I do this to you,
with any part of me you see fit.
Release me and upon command I will have you pulsating,
Gasping for air.
As if you are the survivor of the most pleasurable torture.
On nights when it's cold, warm yourself to me.
I am building now. Far from the well. And it may feel like I will never return,
  But how can one forget a piece of his heart?
  Besides I promised to show you the world
  And so, I have to come back. That's what love does right?
  And I hope when I return we can create what we
  Were always supposed to be,
  What we were designed to do. But that depends.

Are you willing to be naked with me once more?
What say you, best friend?
Soulmate?
In this life and the next will you wait for me?
Or is all of it a mirage?

## ALSO BY NORIAN LOVE

### Novels
Autumn: A Love Story
Money, Power & Sex: A Love Story
Seduction: A Money, Power & Sex Story
Ronnie: A Money Power & Sex Story
Donovan: A Money Power & Sex Novella

### Poetry
Theater of Pain
Games of the Heart
The Dawn or the Dusk

### Music
Autumn: The Soundtrack to the Novel

Made in the USA
Middletown, DE
23 October 2021